Status of
Alaska
Wetlands

Uganik Island, Alaska Peninsula and Southwest Islands
PALUSTRINE OPEN WATER

USFWS

THE AUTHORS

Jonathan V. Hall coordinates the National Wetlands Inventory in the Alaska Region of the U. S. Fish and Wildlife Service.

W. E. Frayer is Dean of the School of Forestry and Wood Products at Michigan Technological University. He specializes in natural resources survey design and analysis.

Bill O. Wilen is Project Leader of the National Wetlands Inventory for the U. S. Fish and Wildlife Service.

DESIGN

Gale Communications; St. Paul, MN

Cover photo: Caribou, Arctic Coastal Plain
PALUSTRINE EMERGENT - FLOODED
BP EXPLORATION (ALASKA) INC.

Back cover photo: Yellow pond lily,
Cook Inlet - Susitna Lowland
S GALE

U.S. Fish and Wildlife Service
Alaska Region
Anchorage, Alaska

ACKNOWLEDGMENTS

This report is the result of extensive effort. Special appreciation is extended to U. S. Fish and Wildlife Service personnel including Don Woodard, Becky Stanley, Tom Dahl, Norm Mangrum, and Rene Whitehead of the National Wetlands Inventory Group, St. Petersburg, Florida; Charles Storrs of the Division of Habitat Conservation, Atlanta, Georgia; and David Dall of the National Wetlands Inventory, Washington, D. C.

Many individuals from Geonex Inc. were responsible for photo interpretation and map production. Principal among these are Keith Patterson, Sheila Ricardi, Marsha Martin, Todd Neurminger, Barbara Schuster, Jim Dick, and Dave Fink. Their work is greatly appreciated.

Funding support from the U. S. Army Corps of Engineers and the National Oceanic and Atmospheric Administration's National Marine Pollution Program Office is gratefully acknowledged. Glen Yankus of the U. S. Department of Interior's Minerals Management Service also assisted in the study.

Status of
Alaska
Wetlands

by Jonathan V. Hall, W. E. Frayer and Bill O. Wilen

1994

Arctic Coastal Plain

BP EXPLORATION (ALASKA) INC

PALUSTRINE OPEN WATER AND EMERGENT - FLOODED

Contents

left: Safety Harbor, Western Coastal Zone
ESTUARINE INTERTIDAL VEGETATED
J. HALL

Mountain cranberry, Kuskokwim Highlands
PALUSTRINE SCRUB/SHRUB - SATURATED
D. DALL

CHAPTER ONE

Introduction

The United States Fish and Wildlife Service has major responsibility for the protection and management of migratory and endangered fish and wildlife and their habitats. Of particular concern are wetlands and associated deepwater habitats. Since 1974 the Fish and Wildlife Service, through its National Wetlands Inventory Project, has inventoried the nation's wetlands. The purpose is to develop and disseminate comprehensive data concerning the characteristics and extent of wetlands.

Results of a National Wetlands Inventory study of wetland gains and losses in the lower 48 states between the 1950's and 1970's were published by Frayer et al. (1983) and Tiner (1984). Of the wetlands at the time of settlement in the area now comprising the 48 contiguous states, only 46 percent remained in the mid-1970's. Between the mid-1950's and mid-1970's, there was a loss of about 11 million acres of wetlands. During the same period, approximately two million acres of wetlands were created. This 20-year net loss of nine million acres equates to an average annual net loss of 458,000 acres of wetlands. An update of this report for the nine-year period between 1974 and 1983 showed the wetland loss rate was down to an average annual net loss of 290,200 acres (Dahl et al. 1991; Frayer 1991).

The statistical design used in the trend study for the lower 48 states can be used with intensified sampling to obtain reliable estimates for individual states or other selected geographical areas. For example, this approach was used to evaluate wetland trends in the Central Valley of California (Frayer and Peters 1990) and Florida (Frayer and Hefner 1992).

This report presents results of a study on the status of wetlands and deepwater habitats in Alaska. This is the first report for Alaska. While it provides estimates of current status of Alaska wetlands and deepwater habitats, it does not provide information on their trends and quality. It does, however, provide information on the amounts of these areas managed by several federal agencies, the State of Alaska, Natives and others.

left: Oil pipeline, Arctic Coastal Plain
PALUSTRINE EMERGENT · FLOODED
J. HALL

*right: Shaw Creek Flats,
Tanana-Kuskokwim Lowland*
PALUSTRINE SCRUB/SHRUB
AND EMERGENT · FLOODED

F. GOLET

CHAPTER TWO

Overview

Wetlands in Alaska include types commonly referred to as bogs, muskegs, wet and moist tundra, fens, marshes, swamps, mud flats, and salt marshes. The U.S. Fish and Wildlife Service estimates that during the 200-year period between 1780 and 1980, approximately 1/10 of a percent of the original wetland acreage in Alaska was lost (Dahl 1990).

Common terms used for Alaska's deepwater habitats include lakes, bays, sounds, fjords, lagoons, and inlets. The two largest lakes in Alaska are Lake Iliamna (1,000 square miles) and Becharof Lake (458 square miles). Large coastal deepwater habitats include Kotzebue Sound, Norton Sound, Bristol Bay, Cook Inlet, and the labyrinth of fjords, inlets, and straits in the Alexander Archipelago (southeast Alaska). Lagoons formed behind barrier islands are common in northwest Alaska along the Chukchi Sea and Bering Strait coasts.

Most regions of Alaska have a land surface that includes extensive areas of wetlands. Treeless expanses of moist and wet tundra underlain by permafrost occur in the northern and western portions. Interior Alaska contains millions of acres of black spruce muskeg and floodplain wetlands dominated by deciduous shrubs and emergents. Shrub and herbaceous bogs are a conspicuous feature of the landscape in south central and southeast Alaska. Even in mountainous areas such as the Brooks Range, wetlands have developed in drainages and on vegetated slopes. Some of the nation's most extensive complexes of salt marshes and mud flats occur along the coasts of the Beaufort Sea, Chukchi Sea, Bering Sea and the Gulf of Alaska.

left: Blying Sound, South Central Coastal Zone
MARINE INTERTIDAL.
J. HALL

Wetlands are abundant in the valleys and basins associated with large river systems including the Yukon, Kuskokwim, Porcupine, Tanana, and Koyukuk Rivers. Significant wetland areas also occur on the major river deltas in Alaska. The Yukon-Kuskokwim Delta, one of the world's largest coastal deltaic formations, supports a variety of wetland types including wet tundra, grassy sloughs, shrub swamps, ponds and brackish marsh. Other major deltas in Alaska that are predominantly wetland are the Colville River Delta on the Beaufort Sea coast, the Copper River Delta in south central Alaska, and the Stikine River Delta in the southeast region.

Many wetlands in northern portions of Alaska are underlain and maintained by permafrost, or perennially frozen ground. Wetland conditions often occur because the frozen layer traps water at or near the soil surface. Other wetlands are maintained by heavy rainfall, glacial melt water, river flooding, beaver activity, snow melt, springs, and the ebb and flow of tides.

Wetlands in Alaska range in elevation from tidal systems at sea level to moist tundra areas in high alpine zones. Wetlands are as common on slopes as they are in lowland sites and depressions. While north-facing slopes are frequently wetland due to the presence of permafrost, south-facing slopes in the same area often support non-wetland plant communities on well-drained soils. Hillside wetlands are common in southern portions of Alaska due to abundant precipitation and shallow depths to bedrock.

Alaska's wetlands provide many benefits including: food and habitat for wildlife, fish and shellfish species, natural products for human use and subsistence, shoreline erosion and sediment control, flood protection, and opportunities for recreation and aesthetic appreciation. Not all wetlands perform all these functions, but most wetlands contribute to one or more in varying degrees.

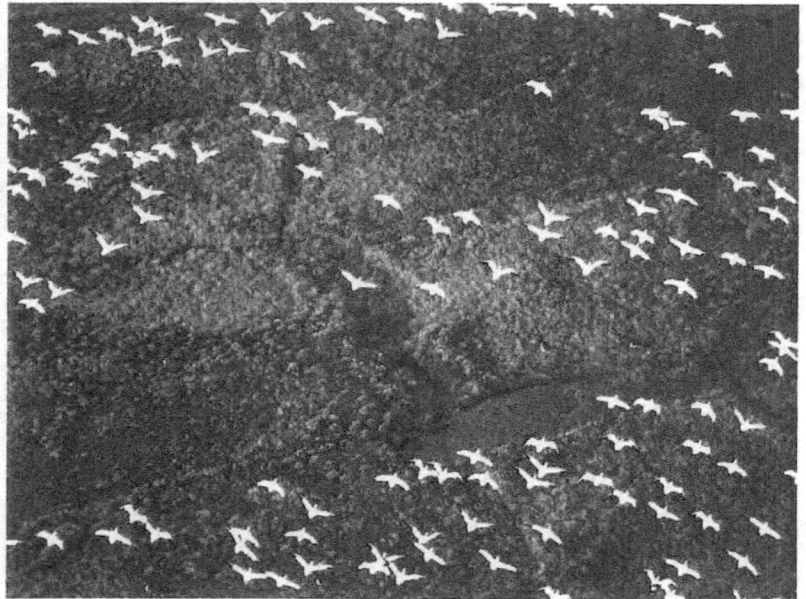

Tundra wetlands in northern and western Alaska are prime breeding grounds for many shorebirds (sandpipers, plovers, and their relatives). Waterfowl species dependent on Alaska wetlands include more than 70 thousand swans, one million geese, and 12 million ducks (King and Lensink 1971). These include more than half the continental populations of tundra and trumpeter swans and all or most of the continental populations of eight species or subspecies of geese. In recent years, Alaska wetlands have on average supported 30 percent of the continental populations of northern pintails, 24 percent of American wigeons, 19 percent of scaup, 18 percent of canvasback, and 13 percent of green-winged teal (Lensink and Derksen 1986). The importance of Alaska wetlands to these and other species increases significantly during years when drought occurs in prairie states and provinces.

During migration, huge flocks of waterfowl and shorebirds stop at specific wetland areas for resting and feeding. These critical wetlands provide concentrated food resources necessary to fuel the journey to nesting areas in the spring or southern destinations in the fall. Nearly all of the Pacific Flyway black brant feed on rich eelgrass beds at Izembek Lagoon on the Alaska Peninsula during fall migration (Fish and Wildlife Service 1985).

Many mammals in Alaska use specific wetland types and areas. Some species, such as beaver and muskrat, spend most of their lives in wetlands. Other mammals use wetlands primarily as feeding areas or resting areas. Moose commonly feed on submerged vegetation in deep marshes and shallow ponds. The two largest herds of caribou, both in northern Alaska, gather into huge aggregations and migrate from upland areas to coastal wetland areas in the summer. Uninterrupted moist tundra wetlands in the North Slope coastal plain are used by these animals for calving and feeding. Nonvegetated wetland types such as gravel bars and coastal beaches are used to escape insect harassment.

The value of wetlands for fish is well established for Alaska's coastal wetlands along rivers and streams. Many fish species feed in wetlands or on food produced by wetlands. Coastal wetlands and stream side marshes are used as nursery grounds. Other wetland types adjacent to rivers maintain and regulate stream flow in channels used by fish. Species (e. g., salmon) that move between fresh water and saltwater are dependent on both coastal and riparian wetlands. Annually, the salmon industry in Alaska employs approximately 22,000 people (Alaska Dept. of Fish and Game 1992). The annual value of this fishery to commercial harvesters is $600 million (Alaska Dept. of Education 1991).

Many wetlands serve to temporarily store flood waters, thereby protecting downstream properties from flood damage. The flood storage function also helps to slow the velocity of water, which reduces the water's erosive potential. This function of wetlands becomes increasingly important in Alaska's towns and cities, where development has increased the rate and volume of surface-water runoff and the potential for flood damage. Where permafrost is common, the ability of wetlands to store flood waters is reduced.

Subsistence use of wetland resources in Alaska is extensive. In most areas, wetland habitats provide resources upon which Native village economies are based. A major portion of hunting, fishing, trapping, and gathering activities occurs in wetlands areas (Ellanna and Wheeler 1986). Fish and wildlife resources harvested for subsistence use and dependent on wetlands include five species of salmon, shellfish, ducks, geese, beaver, and otter. Plant materials frequently collected from wetlands include blueberries, cranberries, labrador tea, and willow.

The diversity of plant and animal life in wetlands makes them a valuable resource for nonconsumptive recreation such as wildlife viewing and photography. Wetlands, particularly in urban areas, are valuable in providing other passive recreation opportunities including education, open space, and aesthetic enjoyment. In addition, waterfowl hunting in the United States depends on continued productivity of Alaska's wetlands.

CHAPTER THREE

Classification System

The definitions, classifications and categories of wetlands and deepwater habitats used are those described by Cowardin et al. (1979). In general terms, wetland is land where saturation with water is the dominant factor determining the nature of soil development and the types of plant and animal communities living in the soil and on its surface. Technically, wetlands are lands transitional between terrestrial and aquatic systems where the water table is usually at or near the surface or the land is covered by shallow water. Wetlands must also have one or more of the following three attributes: 1) at least periodically, the land supports predominantly hydrophytes; 2) the substrate is predominantly undrained hydric soil; and 3) the substrate is nonsoil and is saturated with water or covered by shallow water at some time during the growing season of each year.

Deepwater habitats consist of certain permanently flooded lands. In saltwater areas, the separation between wetland and deepwater habitat coincides with the elevation of the extreme low water of spring tide. In other areas, the separation is at a depth of two meters (6.6 feet) below low water. This is the maximum depth in which emergent plants normally grow.

Within the hierarchical structure of classification, wetlands and deepwater habitats are grouped according to systems. A system consists of environments of similar hydrological, geomorphological, chemical, and biological influences. Each

system is further divided by the driving ecological force, such as ebb and flow of tide, and by substrate material and flooding regimes, or on vegetation life form. Groupings of categories were made to accommodate special interests of the study, and to facilitate comparison of results with those of similar studies conducted in other regions of the United States.

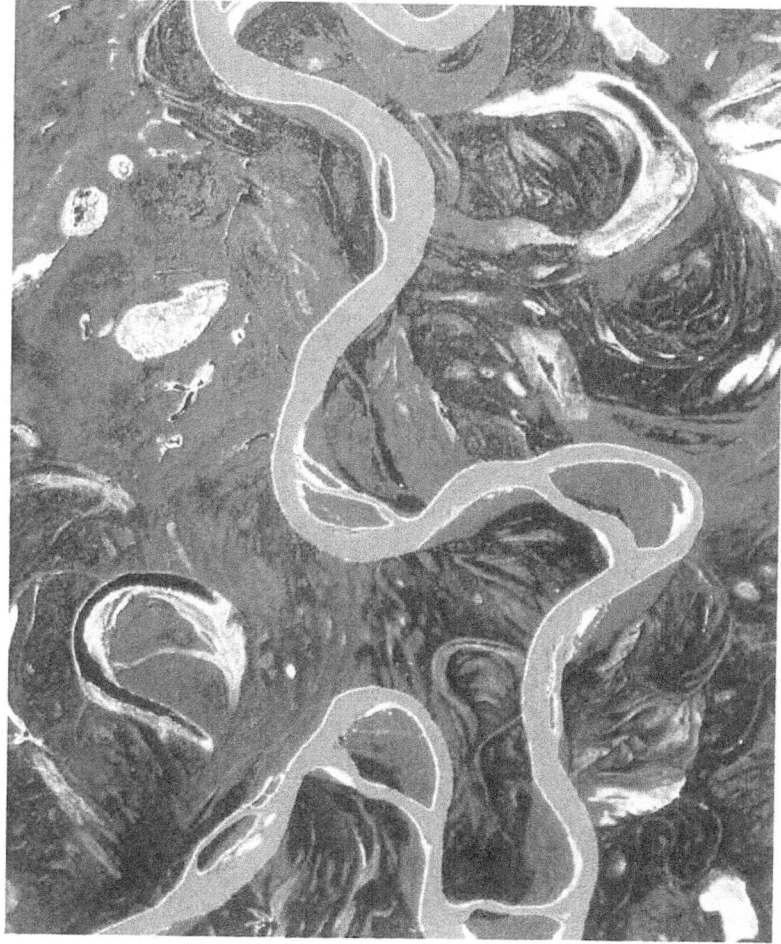

Color-infrared aerial photograph showing Kantishna River, Tanana-Kuskokwim Lowland

The *marine system* extends from the outer edge of the continental shelf shoreward to the extreme high water of spring tides or to the boundary of other systems as defined later. *Marine subtidal* includes that portion that is continuously submerged. This habitat is beyond the scope of the study and was therefore not included. *Marine intertidal* includes areas in which the substrate is exposed and flooded by tides, including the associated splash zone.

The *estuarine system* consists of deepwater tidal habitats and adjacent tidal wetlands which are usually semi-enclosed by land, but have open, partially obstructed, or sporadic access to the open ocean and in which ocean water is at least occasionally diluted by fresh water runoff from the land. *Estuarine subtidal* is that portion that is continuously submerged (considered deepwater habitat), while *estuarine intertidal* is the portion exposed and flooded by tides, including the splash zone. For the purposes of this study, estuarine intertidal wetlands were separated into the following groups: *Nonvegetated*, which includes *unconsolidated shore* (e.g. mud flats) and *aquatic beds* (e.g. seagrasses or algal beds); and *vegetated*,

which is primarily *emergent. Emergent* vegetation consists of erect, rooted herbaceous plants typically found in wet environments.

The *lacustrine system* includes wetlands (littoral) and deepwater habitats (limnetic) situated in topographic depressions or dammed river channels. Each area must exceed 20 acres or be deeper than two meters (6.6 feet) or have an active wave-formed or bedrock shoreline feature. Lacustrine areas are treated as deepwater habitats in this study.

The *palustrine system* includes all nontidal wetlands not included within any of the other four systems and does not include any deepwater habitats. For this study, palustrine wetlands are divided into the following groups: *unconsolidated shore*, *open water* (primarily ponds), *aquatic beds* (e.g. pondlilies and pondweeds), *emergent*, *scrub/shrub*, and *forested. Emergent* is defined the same as for estuarine wetlands. *Forested* is characterized by the presence of trees, and *scrub/shrub* includes areas dominated by shrubs and small or stunted trees.

Yukon-Kuskokwim Delta
PALUSTRINE EMERGENT · FLOODED AND OPEN WATER

F GOLET

Palustrine vegetated wetlands were further separated into categories of *saturated* and *flooded*. *Saturated* wetlands seldom have surface water, but the substrate is saturated for extended periods during the growing season. Wetlands with organic soils, such as bogs, typically are saturated. Other examples of saturated wetlands include moist tundra and black spruce muskegs with permafrost occurring at a shallow depth. *Flooded* wetlands range from temporarily flooded to permanently flooded. In temporarily flooded wetlands, surface water is present for brief periods during the growing season. Flooded wetlands in Alaska include marshes, wet tundra, riparian wetlands, and shrub swamps.

In summary, the 14 wetland and deepwater habitat categories used in this study are:

Category	Common Examples
Marine intertidal	Ocean shoreline
Estuarine subtidal	Open water of bays/inlets
Estuarine intertidal nonvegetated	Mud and sand flats/beaches
Estuarine intertidal vegetated	Salt marsh
Palustrine unconsolidated shore	Pond flats/beaches
Palustrine open water	Open water ponds
Palustrine aquatic beds	Floating and submerged aquatic vegetation
Palustrine emergent - saturated	Moist tussock tundra and sedge bogs
Palustrine emergent - flooded	Wet sedge/grass tundra and marshes
Palustrine scrub/shrub - saturated	Moist shrub tundra and shrub bogs/muskegs
Palustrine scrub/shrub - flooded	Shrub swamps
Palustrine forested - saturated	Forested bogs/muskegs
Palustrine forested - flooded	Forested swamps
Lacustrine	Lakes

Near Naknek, Bristol Bay Coastal Plain
PALUSTRINE EMERGENT - FLOODED

J HALL

All remaining surface area (area not classed as wetland or deepwater habitat) corresponds to classes of *agriculture, urban,* and *other* used by Anderson et al. (1976) at their Classification Level I. *Other* includes Anderson's Level I classes of forest land, rangeland, and barren land, as well as lands that had been cleared of vegetation but had not been put to identifiable use.

The type of ownership of wetlands was also determined in the study. For federal ownership, five categories were selected based on the management agency involved. These include the *Bureau of Land Management, Fish and Wildlife Service, National Park Service, Forest Service,* and *other federal* agencies. Additional ownership cate-

gories are *Native, State* and *other*. The results for individual categories are accurate for only one point in time. After transfers of federal land to Native and State ownership are completed, the samples involved in this study could be reclassified by ownership for timely results.

This briefly describes the classification used in this study. It is difficult to differentiate the categories further without introducing highly technical terms. More detailed discussions, exact definitions, and fuller descriptions are provided by Cowardin et al. (1979).

Yukon-Kuskokwim Delta
PALUSTRINE UNCONSOLIDATED SHORE

F. GOLET

CHAPTER FOUR

Survey Procedure

The objective of the study was to develop statistical estimates of the areal extent of wetland and deepwater habitat categories and ownership classes for Alaska.

A stratified random sampling design was used with 21 inland strata formed by modification of the land resource areas described by Rieger et al. (1979). The study also used four coastal strata encompassing areas in the marine and estuarine systems. The 25 strata and Alaska's four major regions are shown in the map on page 16.

Sample units were allocated to strata in proportion to expected amounts of wetlands and deepwater habitats as estimated by Fish and Wildlife Service personnel. A pilot study with 500 sample units was conducted to estimate the total number of sample units required for the statewide study.

The total number of sample units used statewide was 2,566.

Each sample unit is a four-square mile area, two miles on each side. The units were plotted on U. S. Geological Survey topographic maps and on aerial photographs. The 1:60,000 scale color-infrared aerial photography was obtained for the most recent date available. The average date of this photography was 1980, with 90 percent of the photos within three years of the average.

The photography was interpreted and annotated in accordance with the classification system described earlier and with procedures developed by the Fish and Wildlife Service's National Wetlands Inventory Project. A minimum mapping size of one-half acre was used. Land ownership/management determinations were made from land information records maintained by the Bureau of Land Management.

Kisaralik Lake, Kuskokwim Highlands
LACUSTRINE

D. DALL

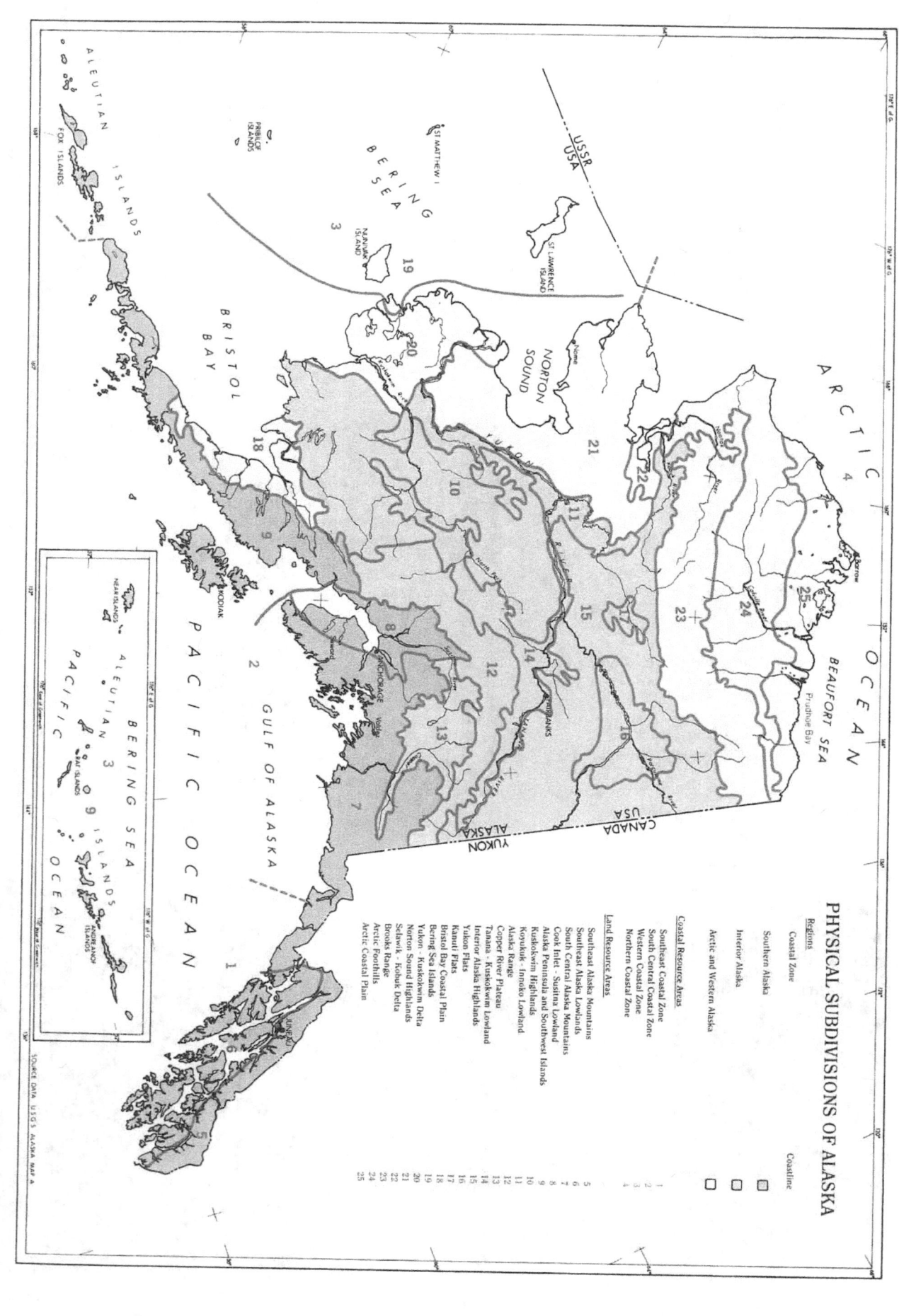

PHYSICAL SUBDIVISIONS OF ALASKA

Regions

Coastal Zone

Southern Alaska

Interior Alaska

Arctic and Western Alaska

Coastal Resource Areas

Southeast Coastal Zone
South Central Coastal Zone
Western Coastal Zone
Northern Coastal Zone

Land Resource Areas

Southeast Alaska Mountains
Southeast Alaska Lowlands
South Central Alaska Mountains
Cook Inlet - Susitna Lowland
Alaska Peninsula and Southwest Islands
Kuskokwim Highlands
Koyukuk - Innoko Lowland
Alaska Range
Copper River Plateau
Tanana - Kuskokwim Lowland
Interior Alaska Highlands
Yukon Flats
Kanuti Flats
Bristol Bay Coastal Plain
Bering Sea Islands
Yukon - Kuskokwim Delta
Norton Sound Highlands
Selawik - Kobuk Delta
Brooks Range
Arctic Foothills
Arctic Coastal Plain

Coastline

1
2
3
4
5
6
7
8
9
10
11
12
13
14
15
16
17
18
19
20
21
22
23
24
25

SOURCE DATA U.S.G.S. ALASKA MAP A

CHAPTER FIVE

Results

The intent of this study was to quantify areal coverage of wetlands and deepwater habitats for Alaska. Results for all categories discussed in the classification system section are given in the Appendix. Several of the individual categories were grouped based on physical, chemical, and biological similarities and are shown as subtotals. These groupings include the following:

Wetlands __and__ deepwater habitats includes all marine, estuarine, palustrine, and lacustrine classifications.

Wetlands includes marine, estuarine, and palustrine wetlands.

Estuarine wetlands includes all estuarine categories except estuarine subtidal (a deepwater habitat).

Palustrine wetlands includes all palustrine categories.

Palustrine nonvegetated wetlands includes the unconsolidated shore, open water, and aquatic bed categories.

Palustrine vegetated wetlands includes all emergent, scrub/shrub, and forested categories.

Palustrine emergent wetlands, palustrine scrub/shrub wetlands, and *palustrine forested wetlands* include the saturated and flooded categories.

Deepwater habitats includes estuarine subtidal and lacustrine habitats.

Results presented in the remainder of this section are based on information found in the Appendix and other supplementary data.

Alaska Range
PALUSTRINE SCRUB/SHRUB - SATURATED

USFWS

WETLANDS AND DEEPWATER HABITATS

The estimate of wetlands and deepwater habitats is 204,554,300 acres (See figure 1). This represents 50.7 percent of Alaska's surface area. In the lower 48 states, wetlands and deepwater habitats only occupy 9.3 percent of the surface area.

WETLANDS

The estimate of wetlands is 174,683,900 acres. The lower 48 states contain an estimated 103,343,600 acres of wetlands (See figures 2, 3). Figure 4 shows the distribution of Alaska wetlands by region.

Suckling Hills, South Central Alaska Mountains
PALUSTRINE EMERGENT - SATURATED AND OPEN WATER

18

J. HALL

Figure 1

Alaska Wetlands and Deepwater Habitats

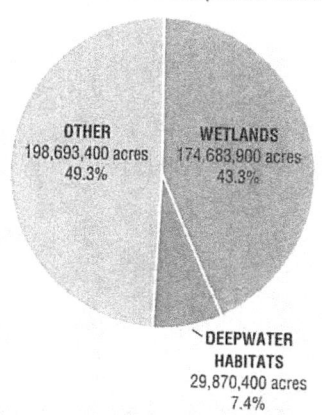

Figures 2, 3

Surface Area of Alaska and Lower 48 States

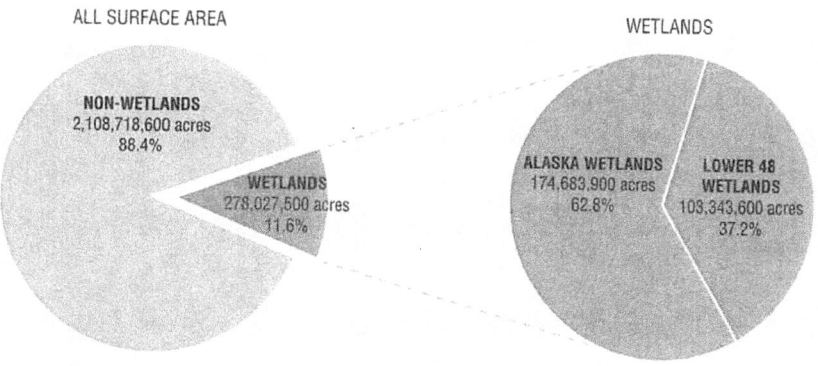

Figure 4

Distribution of Alaska Wetlands by Region

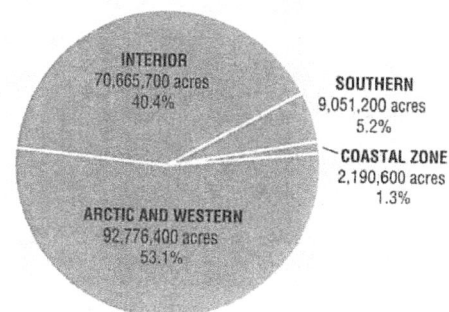

Arctic Foothills
PALUSTRINE EMERGENT - SATURATED

USFWS

The 25 physical subdivisions and four regions appearing in the map on page 16 are shown below with their respective total acreages and wetland areas.

ALASKA PHYSICAL SUBDIVISIONS

PHYSICAL SUBDIVISION	TOTAL ACRES (IN THOUSANDS OF ACRES)	WETLAND ACRES	WETLAND PERCENT
Southeast Alaska Mountains	7,023.9	84.4	1.2
Southeast Alaska Lowlands	11,128.4	3,835.5	34.5
South Central Alaska Mountains	26,375.7	739.4	2.8
Cook Inlet - Susitna Lowland	9,442.0	2,644.5	28.0
Alaska Peninsula & Southwest Islands	15,748.6	1,747.4	11.1
Total - Southern Alaska	**69,718.6**	**9,051.2**	**13.0**
Copper River Plateau	8,367.4	3,056.9	36.5
Alaska Range	18,197.4	1,339.5	7.4
Koyukuk-Innoko Lowland	10,161.0	7,223.0	71.1
Kanuti Flats	1,339.0	1,023.7	76.5
Tanana-Kuskokwim Lowland	13,550.9	8,256.1	60.9
Yukon Flats	9,679.2	3,681.6	38.0
Kuskokwim Highlands	44,182.5	24,462.4	55.4
Interior Alaska Highlands	55,223.7	21,622.5	39.2
Total - Interior Alaska	**160,701.1**	**70,665.7**	**44.0**

PHYSICAL SUBDIVISION	TOTAL ACRES (IN THOUSANDS OF ACRES)	WETLAND ACRES	WETLAND PERCENT
Norton Sound Highlands	34,652.3	18,320.1	52.9
Selawik-Kobuk Delta	3,149.6	2,384.0	75.7
Yukon-Kuskokwim Delta	15,860.3	12,477.0	78.7
Bristol Bay Coastal Plain	6,067.5	3,331.8	54.9
Bering Sea Islands	2,898.1	2,194.5	75.7
Brooks Range	32,406.5	7,182.3	22.2
Arctic Foothills	36,390.6	30,271.1	83.2
Arctic Coastal Plain	20,031.5	16,615.6	82.9
Total - Arctic & Western Alaska	**151,456.4**	**92,776.4**	**61.3**
Southeast Coastal Zone	7,456.8	236.0	3.2
South Central Coastal Zone	6,567.7	694.1	10.6
Western Coastal Zone	3,754.8	1,106.3	29.5
Northern Coastal Zone	3,592.3	154.2	4.3
Total - Coastal Zone[1]	**21,371.6**	**2,190.6**	**10.3**
Total - Alaska	**403,247.7**	**174,683.9**	**43.3**

[1]Coastal Zone acreage is primarily estuarine subtidal, a deepwater habitat

Marine Intertidal Wetlands

The estimate of marine intertidal wetlands is 48,600 acres.

Estuarine Wetlands

The estimate of estuarine wetlands is 2,131,900 acres. This is smaller than the estimated 5,472,700 acres of estuarine wetlands in the lower 48 states (See figure 5). As shown in figures 6 and 7, the majority of estuarine wetlands in Alaska are nonvegetated; the vast majority of estuarine wetlands in the lower 48 states are vegetated. Figure 8 shows the distribution of Alaska estuarine wetlands by coastal subdivisions.

Figure 5

Estuarine Wetlands in Alaska and the Lower 48 States

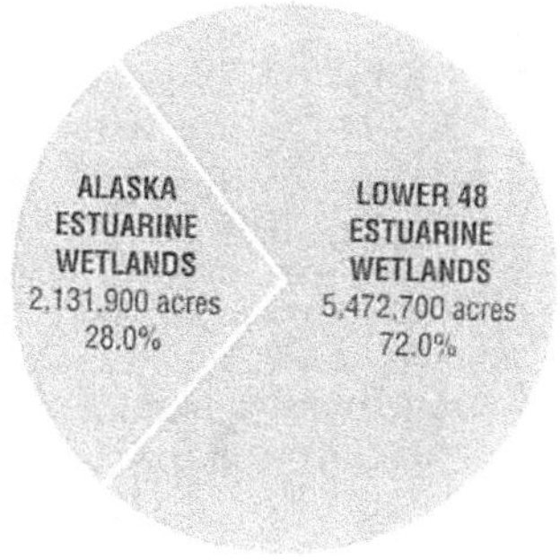

ALASKA ESTUARINE WETLANDS
2,131,900 acres
28.0%

LOWER 48 ESTUARINE WETLANDS
5,472,700 acres
72.0%

Figure 6

Estuarine Wetlands in Alaska

NONVEGETATED
1,771,700 acres
83.1%

VEGETATED
360,200 acres
16.9%

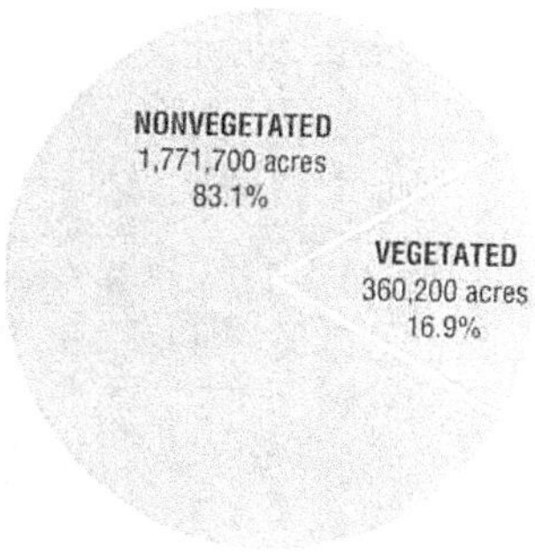

Figure 7

Estuarine Wetlands in the Lower 48 States

VEGETATED
4,782,900 acres
87.4%

NONVEGETATED
689,800 acres
12.6%

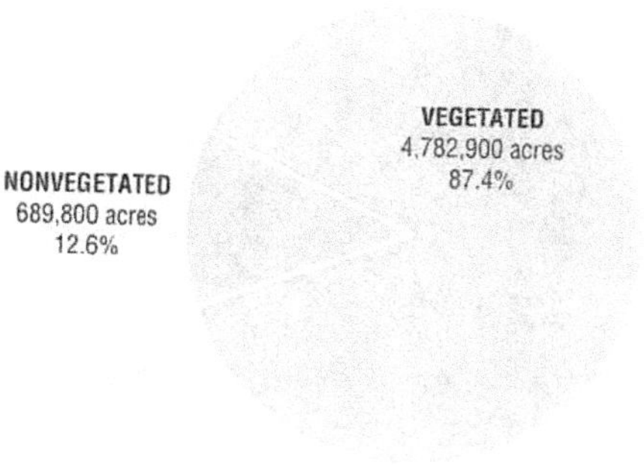

Figure 8

Distribution of Alaska Estuarine Wetlands by Coastal Subdivisions

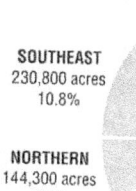

SOUTHEAST
230,800 acres
10.8%

SOUTH CENTRAL
675,900 acres
31.7%

NORTHERN
144,300 acres
6.8%

WESTERN
1,080,900 acres
50.7%

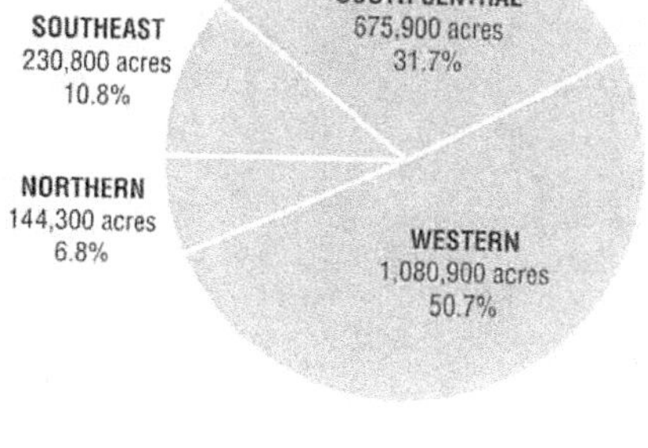

Palustrine Wetlands

The estimate of palustrine wetlands is 172,503,400 acres. This represents 98.8 percent of the wetlands in Alaska.

Palustrine Nonvegetated Wetlands

The estimate of palustrine nonvegetated wetlands in Alaska is 2,670,200 acres. The lower 48 states have 6,141,300 acres of palustrine nonvegetated wetlands. In both cases, most of the area is open water ponds. However, in the mid-1950's, there was only an estimated 2,704,400 acres of palustrine nonvegetated wetlands in the lower 48 states. Most of the increase is due to pond construction.

Palustrine Vegetated Wetlands

The estimate of palustrine vegetated wetlands is 169,833,200 acres. This is much larger than the 91,625,300 acres in the lower 48 states (See figure 9). The distribution is quite different for the two areas. In Alaska, the vast majority of palustrine vegetated wetlands are scrub/shrub wetlands, and the smallest amount is forested wetlands (See figure 10); in the lower 48 states, the majority of palustrine vegetated wetlands are forested wetlands, and the smallest amount is scrub/shrub wetlands (See figure 11). The distribution of palustrine vegetated wetlands in Alaska's Southern, Interior, and Arctic and Western regions is shown in figures 12, 13, and 14, respectively.

Caribou herd, Arctic Coastal Plain
PALUSTRINE EMERGENT - FLOODED

Figure 9

Palustrine Vegetated Wetlands in Alaska and the Lower 48 States

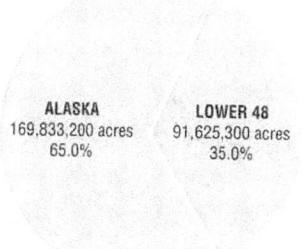

ALASKA
169,833,200 acres
65.0%

LOWER 48
91,625,300 acres
35.0%

Figure 10

Palustrine Vegetated Wetlands in Alaska

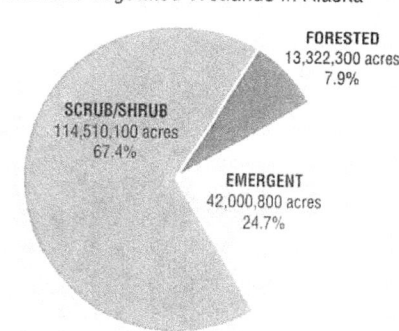

FORESTED
13,322,300 acres
7.9%

SCRUB/SHRUB
114,510,100 acres
67.4%

EMERGENT
42,000,800 acres
24.7%

Figure 11

Palustrine Vegetated Wetlands in the Lower 48 States

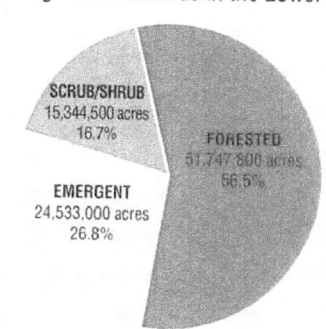

SCRUB/SHRUB
15,344,500 acres
16.7%

FORESTED
51,747,800 acres
56.5%

EMERGENT
24,533,000 acres
26.8%

Figures 12, 13, 14

Palustrine Vegetated Wetlands by Region

SOUTHERN

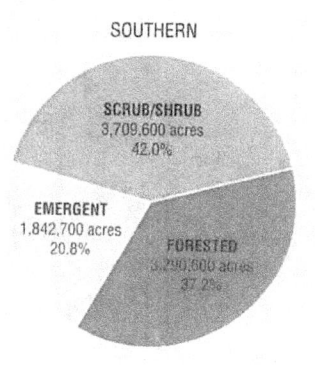

SCRUB/SHRUB
3,709,600 acres
42.0%

EMERGENT
1,842,700 acres
20.8%

FORESTED
3,290,600 acres
37.2%

INTERIOR

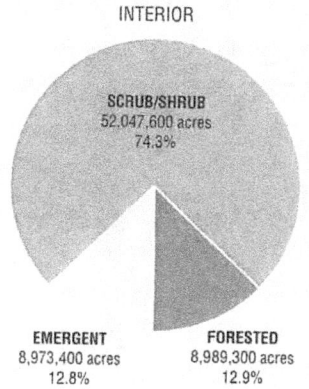

SCRUB/SHRUB
52,047,600 acres
74.3%

EMERGENT
8,973,400 acres
12.8%

FORESTED
8,989,300 acres
12.9%

ARCTIC & WESTERN

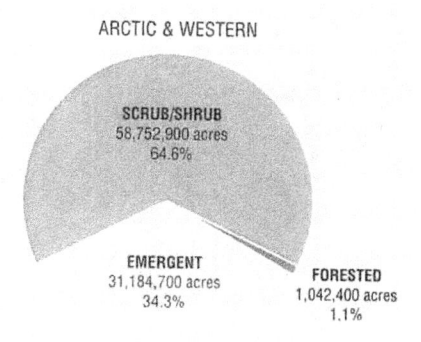

SCRUB/SHRUB
58,752,900 acres
64.6%

EMERGENT
31,184,700 acres
34.3%

FORESTED
1,042,400 acres
1.1%

Palustrine Emergent Wetlands
(Figures 15, 16)

The estimate of palustrine emergent wetlands is 42,000,800 acres. The amounts of saturated and flooded wetlands are approximately equal. Palustrine emergent wetlands are most common in Arctic and Western Alaska, where three-fourths of this type of wetland is found. Over 14 million acres of palustrine emergent wetlands are found in the Arctic Coastal Plain, the only physical subdivision in Alaska with the majority of its surface area in this single type. Over five million acres of palustrine emergent wetlands are found in the Yukon-Kuskokwim Delta and also in the Arctic Foothills.

Palustrine Scrub/Shrub Wetlands
(Figures 17, 18)

The estimate of palustrine scrub/shrub wetlands is 114,510,100 acres. Only 5.8 percent of these wetlands are classified as flooded. Flooded palustrine scrub/shrub wetlands are most common in the Yukon-Kuskokwim Delta, where about one-fourth of the palustrine scrub/shrub wetlands are flooded. Almost 97 percent of the palustrine scrub/shrub wetlands are found in Interior Alaska and Arctic and Western Alaska. Subdivisions having the most palustrine scrub/shrub wetlands are the Arctic Foothills in Arctic and Western Alaska, with 24,548,300 acres; and, the Kuskokwim Highlands and the Interior Alaska Highlands in Interior Alaska with 18,858,900 acres and 16,348,900 acres, respectively.

Palustrine Forested Wetlands
(Figures 19, 20)

The estimate of palustrine forested wetlands is 13,322,300 acres. Only 204,300 acres are classified as flooded. As shown earlier, palustrine forested wetlands cover relatively little area in Alaska compared to the lower 48 states, where it is the most abundant type of wetland.

Tanana-Kuskokwim Lowland
PALUSTRINE SCRUB/SHRUB - FLOODED

F. GOLET

Figures 15, 16

Palustrine Emergent Wetlands

SATURATED VS. FLOODED

DISTRIBUTION BY REGION

SATURATED
21,170,500 acres
50.4%

FLOODED
20,830,300 acres
49.6%

INTERIOR
8,973,400 acres
21.4%

SOUTHERN
1,842,700 acres
4.4%

ARCTIC AND WESTERN
31,184,700 acres
74.2%

Figures 17, 18

Palustrine Scrub/Shrub Wetlands

SATURATED VS. FLOODED

DISTRIBUTION BY REGION

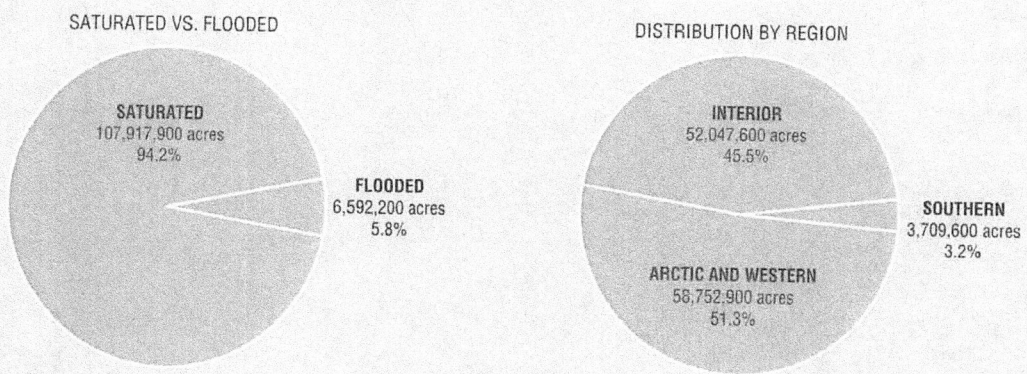

SATURATED
107,917,900 acres
94.2%

FLOODED
6,592,200 acres
5.8%

INTERIOR
52,047,600 acres
45.5%

SOUTHERN
3,709,600 acres
3.2%

ARCTIC AND WESTERN
58,752,900 acres
51.3%

Figures 19, 20

Palustrine Forested Wetlands

SATURATED VS. FLOODED

DISTRIBUTION BY REGION

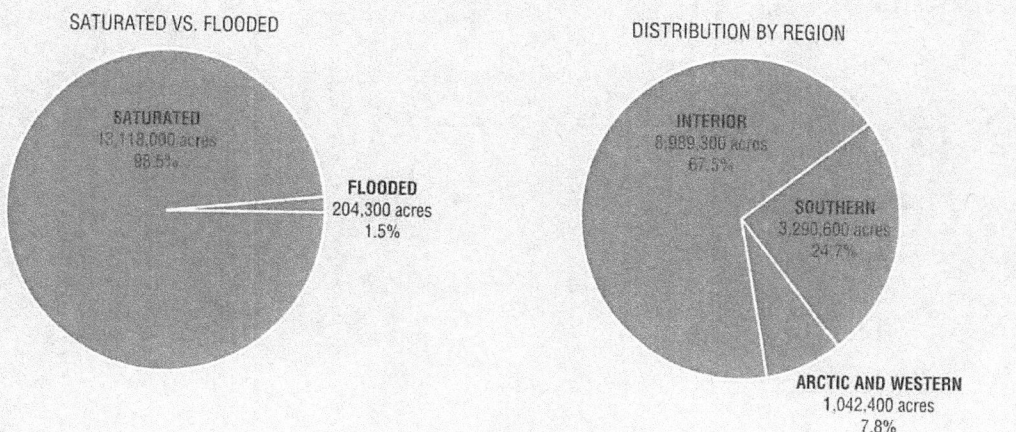

SATURATED
13,118,000 acres
98.5%

FLOODED
204,300 acres
1.5%

INTERIOR
8,989,300 acres
67.5%

SOUTHERN
3,290,600 acres
24.7%

ARCTIC AND WESTERN
1,042,400 acres
7.8%

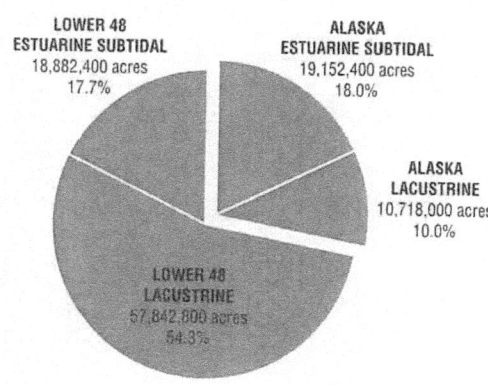

Figure 21
Estuarine and Lacustrine Deepwater Habitats
in Alaska and the Lower 48 States

LOWER 48
ESTUARINE SUBTIDAL
18,882,400 acres
17.7%

ALASKA
ESTUARINE SUBTIDAL
19,152,400 acres
18.0%

ALASKA
LACUSTRINE
10,718,000 acres
10.0%

LOWER 48
LACUSTRINE
57,842,600 acres
54.3%

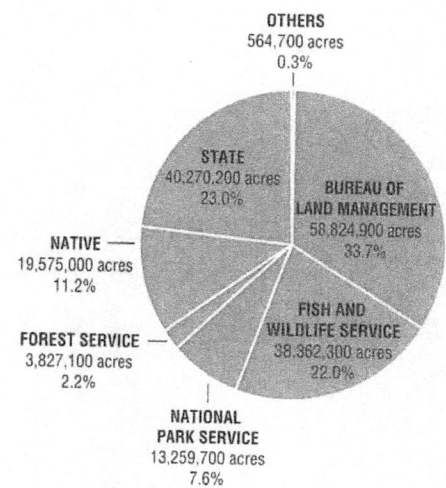

Figure 22
Distribution of Wetlands by Ownership/Management

OTHERS
564,700 acres
0.3%

STATE
40,270,200 acres
23.0%

BUREAU OF
LAND MANAGEMENT
58,824,900 acres
33.7%

NATIVE
19,575,000 acres
11.2%

FOREST SERVICE
3,827,100 acres
2.2%

FISH AND
WILDLIFE SERVICE
38,362,300 acres
22.0%

NATIONAL
PARK SERVICE
13,259,700 acres
7.6%

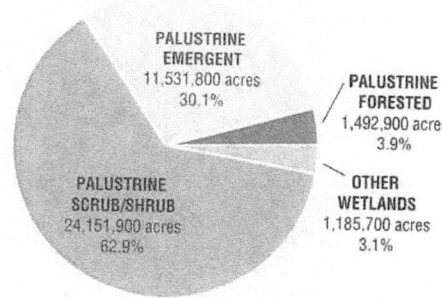

Figure 23
Wetlands under Management by Fish and Wildlife Service

PALUSTRINE
EMERGENT
11,531,800 acres
30.1%

PALUSTRINE
FORESTED
1,492,900 acres
3.9%

PALUSTRINE
SCRUB/SHRUB
24,151,900 acres
62.9%

OTHER
WETLANDS
1,185,700 acres
3.1%

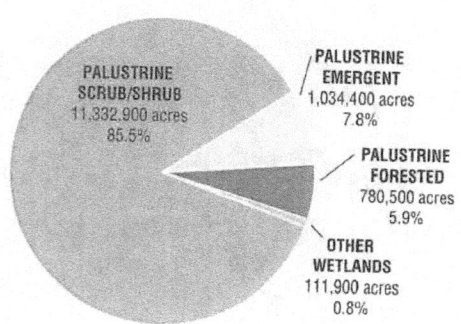

Figure 24
Wetlands under Management by National Park Service

PALUSTRINE
SCRUB/SHRUB
11,332,900 acres
85.5%

PALUSTRINE
EMERGENT
1,034,400 acres
7.8%

PALUSTRINE
FORESTED
780,500 acres
5.9%

OTHER
WETLANDS
111,900 acres
0.8%

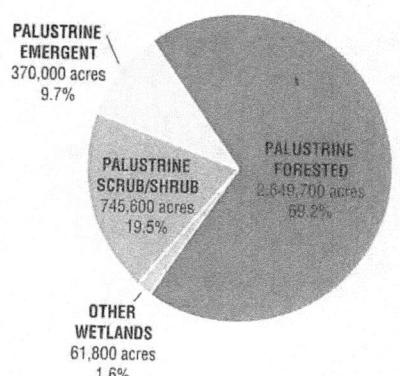

Figure 25
Wetlands under Management by Forest Service

PALUSTRINE
EMERGENT
370,000 acres
9.7%

PALUSTRINE
SCRUB/SHRUB
745,600 acres
19.5%

PALUSTRINE
FORESTED
2,649,700 acres
69.2%

OTHER
WETLANDS
61,800 acres
1.6%

DEEPWATER HABITATS

The estimate of deepwater habitats is 29,870,400 acres. Estuarine subtidal habitats cover approximately the same surface area in Alaska as in the lower 48 states (See figure 21). Alaska has much less acreage in lacustrine deepwater habitats than the lower 48 states; however, about two-thirds of the lacustrine area in the lower 48 states is in the Great Lakes.

OWNERSHIP

The detailed ownership information collected during the study is presented in the summary table in the Appendix. The information should be used with caution, because the State of Alaska and Natives are continuing to receive lands selected from the block of lands managed by the Bureau of Land Management. This results in major shifts in wetland acreages managed by the affected groups. Other shifts have occurred between groups due to land trades and acquisitions, and conversion of State lands to private ownership through homesteading and agricultural programs.

Figure 22 shows the distribution of wetlands among ownership/management categories. The remaining figures show acreages for wetland categories managed by the Fish and Wildlife Service, the National Park Service, and the Forest Service. Acreages in these groups have been relatively stable over the past several years. As might be expected, 1) the Fish and Wildlife Service is managing a greater proportion of emergent wetlands than the other two agencies, and 2) the most prevalent wetland category under Forest Service management is palustrine forested.

Northwestern Lagoon, South Central Coastal Zone
ESTUARINE SUBTIDAL

J HALL

CHAPTER SIX

In Conclusion

This survey provides an estimate of 174,683,900 acres of wetlands in Alaska, dominated by palustrine vegetated wetlands. Alaska contains 63 percent of the total wetland acreage in the United States (excluding Hawaii). While widespread wetland losses have been relatively low in Alaska, specific localities have sustained significant losses (Alaska Dept. of Natural Resources 1993).

Results of this study provide the basis for future studies of wetland trends. One of the first trends that could be studied is the change in the ownership/management of wetlands resulting from continuing land transfers involving federal agencies, Natives, and the State of Alaska. The sample units used in this study could be reclassified by ownership at some future date to provide more current information.

Continual monitoring of surface area use and changes in use is needed to provide the basis for wise decisions. This report is the result of one such method of monitoring initiated by the U. S. Fish and Wildlife Service. The results in this report provide wetland information similar to 1) the forest and range information required by the Forest and Rangeland Renewable Resources Planning Act, and 2) information on soil, water, and related resources required by the Soil and Water Resource Conservation Act. The results can be updated in the future on the schedule required by those Acts.

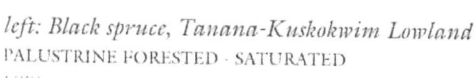

left: Black spruce, Tanana-Kuskokwim Lowland
PALUSTRINE FORESTED - SATURATED
J HALL

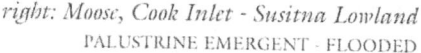

right: Moose, Cook Inlet - Susitna Lowland
PALUSTRINE EMERGENT - FLOODED

USFWS

Literature Cited

Alaska Department of Commerce and Economic Development. 1992. Seafood Industry Sector Report. State of Alaska, Dept. of Commerce and Econ. Dev., Div. of Business Dev. 181 pp.

Alaska Department of Education. 1991. Alaska Blue Book 1991-1992, Ninth Ed. State of Alaska, Dept. of Educ., Div. of State Libraries, Archives, and Museums. 369 pp.

Alaska Department of Natural Resources. 1993. Alaska's outdoor legacy: statewide comprehensive outdoor recreation plan, 1992-1996. State of Alaska, Dept. of Natural Resources. 80 pp.

Anderson, James R., Ernest E. Hardy, John T. Roach, and Richard E. Witmer. 1976. A land use and cover classification system for use with remote sensor data. U. S. Geol. Surv. Prof. Paper 964. 22 pp.

Cowardin, L. M., V. Carter, F. C. Golet, and E. T. LaRoe. 1979. Classification of wetlands and deepwater habitats of the United States. U. S. Fish Wildl. Serv. 103 pp.

Dahl, T. E. 1990. Wetland losses in the United States, 1780's to 1980's. U. S. Fish Wildl. Serv. 21 pp.

Dahl, T. E., and C. E. Johnson. 1991. Status and trends of wetlands in the conterminous United States, mid-1970's to mid-1980's. U. S. Fish Wildl. Serv. 28 pp.

Ellanna, L. J., and P. C. Wheeler. 1986. Subsistence use of wetlands in Alaska. In: Alaska Regional Wetland Functions - Proceedings of a Workshop. The Environmental Institute, Univ. of Mass. pp 85-103.

Frayer, W. E., T. J. Monahan, D. C. Bowden, and F. A. Graybill. 1983. Status and trends of wetlands and deepwater habitats in the conterminous United States, 1950's to 1970's. Colo. State Univ. 32 pp.

Frayer, W. E., and Dennis Peters. 1989. Wetlands of the California Central Valley: Status and trends, 1939 to mid-1980's. U. S. Fish Wildl. Serv. 28 pp.

Frayer, W. E. 1991. Status and trends of wetlands and deepwater habitats in the conterminous United States, 1970's to 1980's. Mich. Technological Univ. 32 pp.

Frayer, W. E., and John Hefner. 1991. Florida wetlands: Status and trends, 1970's to 1980's. U. S Fish Wildl. Serv. 32 pp.

King, J. G., and C. J. Lensink. 1971. An evaluation of Alaska habitat for migratory birds. Unpublished report. Bureau of Sport Fisheries and Wildlife, Wash., D. C. 72 pp.

Lensink, C. J., and D. V. Derksen. 1986. Evaluation of Alaska wetlands for waterfowl. In: Alaska Regional Wetland Functions - Proceedings of a Workshop. The Environmental Institute, Univ. of Mass. pp. 45-84.

Rieger, Samuel, Dale B. Schoephorster and Clarence E. Furbush. 1979. Exploratory soil survey of Alaska. U. S. Dept. Agr. Soil Cons. Serv. 213 pp.

U. S. Fish and Wildlife Service. 1985. Izembek National Wildlife Refuge – comprehensive conservation plan. U. S. Fish Wildl. Serv., Anchorage, Alaska. 270 pp.

left: Stikine River Delta, Southeast Alaska Lowlands
PALUSTRINE EMERGENT - FLOODED
J HALL

Appendix

Estimates produced include acreages with associated standard errors. Many estimates are not considered reliable enough to recommend their use for making decisions. An indication is given of the reliability of each estimated acreage in the summary tables included in this appendix. The standard error of each entry expressed as a percentage of the entry (SE%) is given in parentheses. Reliability can be stated generally as "we are 68 percent confident that the true value is within the interval constructed by adding to and subtracting from the entry the SE%/100 times the entry." For example, if an entry is one million acres and the SE% is 20, then we are 68 percent confident that the true value is between 800,000 and 1,200,000 acres. An equivalent statement for 95 percent confidence can be made by adding and subtracting twice the amount to and from the entry.

Therefore, a large SE% indicates low reliability, if any, in the estimate. In fact, if the SE% is 100 or greater, we cannot even say that we are 68 percent confident that the true value is not zero.

This discussion on reliability is meant to aid in interpretation of the study results. It was expected that only certain estimates would be precise enough to be meaningful. However, all entries are included in the summary table for additivity and ease of comparison.

Estimates were produced for categories described in Chapter Three. These estimates are summarized on the next page. Totals for columns are estimates of total acreage by ownership/management classification category. Row totals (the extreme right column) are estimates of total acreage by surface area category. Entries are interpreted as in the following examples (all from the second and tenth columns of the table):

• • 11,531,800 acres classified as palustrine emergent are managed by the U. S. Fish and Wildlife Service.

• • 42,000,800 acres are classified as palustrine emergent.

• • 24,151,900 acres classified as palustrine scrub/shrub are managed by U. S. Fish and Wildlife Service.

• • The estimate of palustrine forested area is 13,322,300 acres.

• • The estimated area of wetlands and deepwater habitats is 204,554,300 acres.

Seaside plantain,
Anchorage, South Central Coastal Zone
ESTUARINE INTERTIDAL VEGETATED

F. GOLET

TABLE 1. Area, in thousands of acres, by surface area classification.
Sampling error, in percent, is given in parentheses below estimate.

OWNERSHIP CLASSIFICATION

| | FEDERAL | | | | | | | | | |
	BUREAU OF LAND MGMT.	FISH AND WILDLIFE SERVICE	NATIONAL PARK SERVICE	FOREST SERVICE	OTHER FEDERAL	ALL FEDERAL	NATIVE	STATE	OTHER	ALL OWNER-SHIPS
MARINE INTERTIDAL WETLANDS	0	2.9 (42.9)	0	0	0	2.9 (42.9)	0	45.7 (31.1)	0	48.6 (29.7)
ESTUARINE INTERTIDAL — NON-VEGETATED	0.6 (75.2)	58.0 (44.0)	5.2 (72.2)	0.1 (55.0)	1.3 (93.2)	65.2 (39.6)	7.5 (53.2)	1698.0 (7.9)	1.0 (94.9)	1771.7 (7.6)
ESTUARINE INTERTIDAL — VEGETATED	5.6 (45.6)	52.6 (36.3)	0.9 (54.6)	23.6 (46.6)	4.5 (87.0)	87.2 (25.8)	17.0 (37.4)	255.9 (18.2)	0.1 (95.0)	360.2 (14.3)
ESTUARINE WETLANDS	6.2 (41.9)	110.6 (30.3)	6.1 (69.4)	23.7 (46.4)	5.8 (71.8)	152.4 (23.5)	24.5 (33.2)	1953.9 (7.4)	1.1 (94.9)	2131.9 (7.1)
PALUSTRINE — UNCONSOLIDATED SHORE	5.4 (54.6)	15.3 (83.1)	0.1 (81.0)	<0.1 (100.0)	0	20.8 (62.8)	1.0 (58.1)	11.2 (46.3)	0	33.0 (42.5)
PALUSTRINE — OPEN WATER	489.8 (9.4)	992.6 (7.4)	103.3 (20.3)	37.6 (31.0)	0.4 (99.5)	1623.7 (5.4)	549.4 (13.7)	336.4 (10.2)	1.5 (60.7)	2511.0 (4.1)
PALUSTRINE — AQUATIC BEDS	13.1 (30.5)	64.3 (22.8)	2.4 (59.8)	0.5 (55.2)	0	80.3 (18.9)	24.4 (24.2)	20.7 (24.8)	0.8 (99.3)	126.2 (13.4)
NON-VEGETATED	508.3 (9.2)	1072.2 (7.3)	105.8 (20.0)	38.1 (30.1)	0.4 (99.5)	1724.8 (5.4)	574.8 (13.3)	368.3 (10.0)	2.3 (70.3)	2670.2 (4.0)
EMERGENT – SATURATED	8252.2 (10.4)	5956.6 (11.5)	357.1 (57.7)	205.9 (19.6)	0.1 (75.7)	14771.9 (7.4)	1909.2 (16.4)	4483.0 (15.5)	6.4 (66.4)	21170.5 (5.9)
EMERGENT – FLOODED	6582.4 (8.1)	5575.2 (9.2)	677.3 (24.5)	164.1 (78.1)	2.5 (88.7)	13001.5 (5.6)	3229.4 (12.2)	4586.0 (9.8)	13.4 (78.1)	20830.3 (3.9)
EMERGENT	14834.6 (7.4)	11531.8 (8.0)	1034.4 (26.1)	370.0 (36.8)	2.6 (84.1)	27773.4 (5.0)	5138.6 (10.8)	9069.0 (10.3)	19.8 (57.9)	42000.8 (3.5)
SCRUB/SHRUB – SATURATED	38243.3 (5.4)	22132.0 (6.6)	10774.9 (14.3)	683.7 (17.8)	222.2 (52.7)	72056.1 (3.7)	12064.3 (10.4)	23708.9 (7.0)	88.6 (49.2)	107917.9 (2.4)
SCRUB/SHRUB – FLOODED	1372.3 (10.9)	2019.9 (12.5)	558.0 (18.4)	61.9 (55.9)	36.1 (83.6)	4048.2 (7.6)	955.7 (20.8)	1566.3 (10.9)	22.0 (55.8)	6592.2 (5.9)
SCRUB/SHRUB	39615.6 (5.3)	24151.9 (6.3)	11332.9 (14.0)	745.6 (19.5)	258.3 (48.2)	76104.3 (3.6)	13020.0 (10.0)	25275.2 (6.8)	110.6 (49.1)	114510.1 (2.3)
FORESTED – SATURATED	3827.9 (16.2)	1462.8 (16.8)	767.1 (43.5)	2631.2 (11.0)	103.7 (65.8)	8792.7 (8.9)	792.3 (22.1)	3483.9 (12.7)	49.1 (44.4)	13118.0 (6.7)
FORESTED – FLOODED	32.3 (38.2)	30.1 (62.6)	13.4 (62.6)	18.5 (42.4)	2.3 (99.4)	96.6 (26.1)	24.8 (58.5)	74.2 (58.3)	8.7 (76.6)	204.3 (25.7)
FORESTED	3860.2 (16.1)	1492.9 (16.8)	780.5 (42.8)	2649.7 (10.9)	106.0 (64.5)	8889.3 (8.9)	817.1 (22.1)	3558.1 (12.5)	57.8 (42.1)	13322.3 (6.6)
VEGETATED	58310.4 (4.3)	37176.6 (5.2)	13147.8 (13.1)	3765.3 (11.3)	366.9 (44.9)	112767.0 (2.8)	18975.7 (8.5)	37902.3 (5.7)	188.2 (43.3)	169833.2 (1.6)
PALUSTRINE WETLANDS	58818.7 (4.3)	38248.8 (5.1)	13253.6 (13.0)	3803.4 (11.2)	367.3 (44.9)	114491.8 (2.7)	19550.5 (8.5)	38270.6 (5.6)	190.5 (43.5)	172503.4 (1.6)
ALL WETLANDS	58824.9 (4.3)	38362.3 (5.1)	13259.7 (13.0)	3827.1 (11.2)	373.1 (44.2)	114647.1 (2.7)	19575.0 (8.5)	40270.2 (5.4)	191.6 (43.2)	174683.9 (1.5)
ESTUARINE SUBTIDAL	0.7 (64.3)	40.7 (65.1)	<0.1 (95.0)	<0.1 (95.7)	865.2 (14.4)	906.6 (14.0)	3.9 (44.1)	18224.6 (1.0)	17.3 (95.0)	19152.4 (0.8)
LACUSTRINE	2496.5 (12.8)	2733.4 (12.5)	179.6 (28.1)	350.4 (38.5)	0	5759.9 (8.5)	1435.3 (15.7)	3519.7 (17.9)	3.1 (99.2)	10718.0 (7.5)
DEEPWATER HABITATS	2497.2 (12.8)	2774.1 (12.3)	179.6 (28.1)	350.4 (38.5)	865.2 (14.4)	6666.5 (7.6)	1439.2 (15.6)	21744.3 (3.0)	20.4 (82.0)	29870.4 (2.7)
WETLANDS AND DEEPWATER HABITATS	61322.1 (4.2)	41136.4 (5.0)	13439.3 (12.8)	4177.5 (10.2)	1238.3 (16.7)	121313.6 (2.7)	21014.2 (7.9)	62014.5 (3.5)	212.0 (39.9)	204554.3 (1.3)